I WANT TO BE . . . BOOK SERIES
Creator/Producer: Stephanie Maze, Maze Productions
Writer and Educational Consultant: Catherine O'Neill Grace
Designer: Lisa Lytton-Smith

Photographers for I WANT TO BE AN ENGINEER:
Peter Menzel, Cary Wolinsky, Barbara Ries, Karen Kasmauski,
Paul Sancya, Nick Kelsh, Joanna Pinneo, Annie Griffiths Belt,
Richard T. Nowitz, Joe McNally, Joel Sartore, Steve Ringman,
Lara Jo Regan, Bill Tiernan, J. Kyle Keener

Other books in this series:
I WANT TO BE AN ASTRONAUT
I WANT TO BE A DANCER
I WANT TO BE A VETERINARIAN
I WANT TO BE A CHEF
I WANT TO BE A FIREFIGHTER

Requests for permission to make copies
of any part of the work should be mailed to:
Permissions Department, Harcourt Brace & Company,
6277 Sea Harbor Drive, Orlando, Florida 32887-6777.

Library of Congress Cataloging-in-Publication Data
Maze, Stephanie.
I want to be an engineer/by Stephanie Maze and Catherine O'Neill Grace.
p. cm.—(I want to be . . . book series)
Summary: Describes the work of the various branches of engineering.
ISBN 0-15-201298-2
1. Engineering—Vocational guidance—Juvenile literature. 2. Engineers—
Vocational guidance—Juvenile Literature.
[1. Engineers. 2. Occupations.] I. Grace, Catherine O'Neill, 1950–
II. Title. III. Series.
TA157.M3415 1997
620'.0023—dc20 96-26982

ISBN 0-15-202109-4 pb
A C E F D B

Pre-press through PrintNet
Printed and bound by Tien Wah Press, Singapore

I Want to Be...

AN ENGINEER

A Maze Productions Book

HARCOURT BRACE & COMPANY

SAN DIEGO   NEW YORK   LONDON

ACKNOWLEDGMENTS

We wish to thank the following people, companies, and institutions for their very valuable contributions to this book: Henry Petroski, Chair, Department of Civil and Environmental Engineering, Duke University; Jeffrey Leaf, Thomas Jefferson High School for Science and Technology; Mary Paris, Director of Communications, National Society of Professional Engineers; Dan Kunz, Executive Director, Junior Engineering Technical Society (JETS); Greg Pearson, Editor, National Academy of Engineering; Dr. Jay Jaroslav, Research Scientist and Director, Office of Strategic Planning, Artificial Intelligence Laboratory, Massachusetts Institute of Technology; Don L. Everton Jr., Vice President, Norshipco; Anne Perusek, Editor, SWE Magazine; Dawsalee Griffin, The Boeing Company; Janet Staats, Du Pont Company; Ken Vogel, Metropolitan Washington Airports Authority; Kristin Kinley, Ford Motor Company; Darian Germain, Sprint; Nagisa Yamamoto, Industrial Light & Magic; Alana Rothstein, Amalgamated Dynamics, Inc.; Society of Women Engineers; Eric Delony, Historic American Engineering Record; Chuck Blue, National Academy of Engineering; Stephen A. Gates, American Society of Civil Engineers; Mark Monjeau, Project Create; Purdue University; Massachusetts Institute of Technology; George Washington University; Occidental College; Mike Gentry, NASA Media Resource Center, Houston; Dia Stolnitz, U.S. FIRST, The Competition; American Vocational Association; Rick Smolan; Thomas K. Walker, Graf-x, New York; A & I Color Laboratory, Los Angeles.

Many thanks, also, to the very talented people who have participated in the I WANT TO BE . . . project: the photographers, writer Catherine O'Neill Grace, and designer Lisa Lytton-Smith, as well as our colleagues at Harcourt Brace Children's Books, publisher Louise Howton Pelan and editor Karen Weller-Watson, whose guidance has been invaluable.

And finally, our heartfelt gratitude to all the professionals in this book for allowing us to interrupt their busy schedules and for agreeing to be the wonderful role models children can look up to for many years to come.

To all children who dream the impossible dreams

Where to Start

Are you reading this book by the glow of an electric light? The generators, power lines, and circuits that brought the energy into your house to light the bulb were invented, designed, and built by engineers. Do you take a bus to school, carpool, ride your bike, or walk? The design of your bike, the roadway system you travel on, the safety belt or helmet that could save your life in a crash were all developed by engineers. If you log on to a computer when you get to school, you can thank engineers again for designing the hardware and software.

If you like to build things, solve problems, and make systems work better, you could be an engineer. You need to develop your math skills, communication skills, and knowledge of science and logic so that you can work effectively on teams with other problem solvers.

Engineers turn ideas into reality. They solve practical problems with science and technology. Part scientist, part technician, part inventor, an engineer designs and produces things—from roadways to roller coasters, jet engines to juicers, and cars to computer chips.

Computers are central to engineering today. In the picture at right, mechanical engineer Kem D. Alhers uses a computer "virtual reality" system that simulates a test track to check the steering of a huge earthmoving machine called a Caterpillar. The system is located at the National Center for Supercomputing Applications in Champaign, Illinois. Using it, Alhers can maneuver and simulate scooping up gravel while hearing lifelike sounds.

242

Construction Engineer

Code Engineer

Engineers indoors and out. These experts are all hard at work on the same project: building a new terminal at National Airport, near Washington, D.C. Victoria Hankerson reviews plans near the structure (top left). Ray Lum measures a blueprint (top right).

Structural engineer Roderick Hosang checks cables that will be used in constructing the terminal (left). On the site, Gilbert E. Jones keeps in touch with workers (below left). Inside the new terminal, Larry Chandler checks electrical switches and circuits (below).

Safety Engineer

Electrical Engineer

Types of Engineers

Agricultural Engineer

Mechanical Engineer

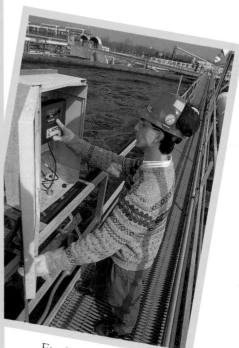

Environmental Engineer

Engineers work on many kinds of problems. At Purdue University in West Lafayette, Indiana, Dirk E. Maier, a professor of biochemical and food processing engineering, analyzes cereal quality (above left). Mechanical and industrial engineer Pete Worth examines pipes in a boiler room that will heat a new terminal building at National Airport near Washington, D.C. (above center). Environmental engineer Mario Vasquez checks water quality at a Du Pont waste treatment plant, where water is cleaned before it flows back into the Delaware River (above right).

Our complex industrial world depends on an amazing array of machines and systems to provide food, water, shelter, and energy; to move people from place to place; and to make instant communication possible. Not only do engineers develop these systems, they keep them running and work to make them better. There are several broad categories of engineers to do all these jobs and many specialists within each category.

Mechanical engineers develop new machinery and adapt old systems for new uses. They make people comfortable by inventing more efficient heating and cooling systems, and they plan ways to make manufacturing processes operate smoothly and safely.

Civil engineers design transportation systems, irrigation systems, and water treatment plants.

They design, build, and maintain bridges and roads. They figure out how to keep airplanes moving safely through the complex air-traffic control system. They may even design amusement park rides.

Electrical engineers design systems and equipment to generate and deliver electricity, including huge dams and tiny computer circuits. They work in electronics, too—on lasers, stereo systems, robots, computers, and worldwide communication networks. They also figure out how to communicate with spacecraft.

Chemical engineers use their knowledge and imagination to invent useful combinations of chemical substances and to synthesize new materials. They devise systems to control pollution, and they work on creating stronger plastics. They also join physicians in their efforts to develop drugs to combat AIDS, cancer, and other illnesses.

Chemical Engineer

Computer Engineer

Within these broad categories there are many, many specialties. The specialists include automotive engineers, who design and build cars, and aerospace engineers, who work on spacecraft. Biotechnology engineers use living things such as bacteria or genes to make or change products and to treat illnesses. Ceramics engineers find methods for transforming sand and clay into products such as computer chips and unbreakable glass.

Construction engineers develop ways to make buildings tall and functional as well as energy efficient and resistant to natural forces such as earthquakes and hurricanes. Environmental engineers devise production methods that pollute the environment as little as possible, and they find ways to clean up the messes that outdated manufacturing and transportation systems leave behind. Fire protection engineers develop methods to fight fires more successfully. Naval engineers design ships. Plastics engineers make stronger, lighter materials and work to improve recycling.

Engineers will be important shapers of the world in the twenty-first century. Do you want to get involved?

Astronautical and aeronautical engineer G. David Low inspects equipment retrieved during a space shuttle flight (large photo). Vinita C. Goel checks pressure gauges on chemical tanks at a Du Pont plant in Delaware (top left). At a biotechnology lab in Austria, an engineer in a sterile suit adjusts a dial (top right). Computer engineer Alan Rock tests software at United Industrial in Maryland (bottom left). At a Mobil Oil facility in New Jersey, a plastics engineer monitors a recycling vat (bottom right).

Biotechnology Engineer

Plastics Engineer

Engineering a Car

The Ford Mustang has been a dream car for millions of motorists since it was first introduced in 1964. An automobile that sported the logo of a galloping pony—a symbol of freedom and excitement (above)—the Mustang almost instantly became one of the top five automobiles in the United States. During the first four months that it was available, it had a hundred thousand buyers! The Ford Motor Company engineers had worked hard at the Dearborn, Michigan, headquarters to create the car, and they had a lot to celebrate. Then they went right back to their plans, models, and test laboratories to work on making the Mustang more powerful, more efficient, and safer.

Engineers have been involved in every step of Mustang production—from design to manufacturing and safety testing. Improvements on the Mustang continue today with the help of high-tech equipment that car designers in the 1960s didn't dream of. Above, product design engineer Lisa Cratty and designer Paul Arnone work at a paintbox computer as they dream up a Ford Mustang for the twenty-first century.

Making Mustangs. *Cars move through various phases of production at a Ford plant in Dearborn, Michigan. Sparks fly (top left) as robotic spot-welding machines piece together the unpainted steel parts of a Mustang body. Charles Nason (top right), who has worked building Mustangs for nearly thirty years, operates machinery that lifts engines into the car bodies moving by overhead. Above, engine-cooling system development engineer Terry Ahluwalia (standing) works with product technicians Floyd Stanley (left) and Stephen Fields as they attach exhaust extraction pipes to a car. The team of experts is about to run a test to see how well the Mustang's engine functions at high temperatures.*

Education and Training

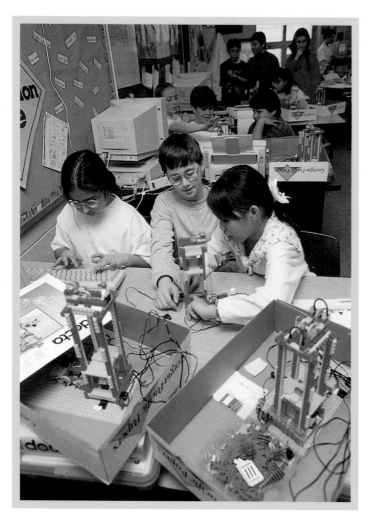

"Techies" at work. *At Crossfield Elementary School in Fairfax, Virginia, students work in teams to solve problems and build models. The school is the site of a pilot research program to promote technology in elementary schools.*

Are you curious? Are you the kind of person who takes things apart to find out how they work? When an airplane flies overhead, do you wonder what keeps it in the air? When you ride an elevator to the thirty-fifth floor of a skyscraper, do you visualize the pulleys that are carrying you through vertical space?

If you answered yes to any of these questions, you're already thinking like an engineer. The next step is to find programs that give you hands-on experience in solving problems by using your curiosity, your imagination, and your intelligence. (A little math and science will help, too.) That's what the kids on these pages are doing— although it may look like they're simply having fun tinkering with things. They're participating in real life experiences in engineering, from building houses to figuring out how everyday objects such as mixers, juicers, and computers work. In the large photo at right, fifth graders from Beverly Farms Middle School in Potomac, Maryland, are taking part in a school program at the National Building Museum in Washington, D.C. It's called "If I Had a Hammer." Students use tools to put together a prefabricated house from the ground up. As they work they explore the basics of structure and design. They learn about foundations, building materials, and tools. And at the end of just two hours, they have the satisfaction of walking around in a house they have constructed themselves.

To enter the professional world of engineering, you need education. After high school, you might enter an engineering program at a four-year college. You might consider a two-year course of study that prepares you to work as a technician in one of the branches of the field, such as electrical or chemical engineering.

Thomas Jefferson High School for Science and Technology in Fairfax, Virginia, has many well-equipped laboratories, where students study disciplines such as computer-aided design, microelectronics, and biotechnology. "TJ" students are also paired with mentors who are technology professionals in industry and universities. Teacher Jeffrey Leaf (above left in tie) helps some students in a mechanical engineering class explore the electronic components of everyday objects— including a sewing machine—while other students take apart a VCR (above right).

Or you might consider a co-op program that lets you work as a technician in an engineering profession while earning your degree.

Engineers use their knowledge of math, science, and technology to solve problems and to create new systems or machinery. They plan and design projects from concept to completion. This process involves making calculations and drafting plans.

Today pursuing any scientific or technical career—but especially engineering—means understanding and being comfortable with computers and computer programming. Engineering study includes working on computers to create statistical and mathematical models of new ideas. Engineers-in-training also use computer-aided design (CAD) to draft blueprints of equipment they want to build or to create flow charts of projects they want to do. But it isn't enough just to have a great blueprint of an idea on a computer printout; engineers have to be able to build things, too. And the things they build have to work!

To develop the technical skills they need, engineering students learn by doing. Above far left, many hands organize electrical wires at the Electronic Data Systems Internship Program for Chantilly High School students in Chantilly, Virginia. Above center, students in a two-year engineering program at Northern Virginia Community College in Annandale, Virginia, work on a circuit board under the guidance of professor Rassa Rassai. Above right, Stephanie LaRue of Purdue University in Indiana machines parts for a car. These students' hands-on experiences give them the mechanical skills they need to turn their ideas into reality.

Putting it together. At right, Massachusetts Institute of Technology student Jerry Pratt works on a robot called Spring Turkey in the Artificial Intelligence Lab in Cambridge, Massachusetts. The robot simulates the way a bird walks. Below, student Michael Hobson works on a "mini-baja," a land/water vehicle. Hobson is enrolled in the mechanical engineering department at Purdue University in West Lafayette, Indiana.

Competitions

Each year inventive engineers in elementary schools, middle schools, high schools, and colleges enter a variety of technology competitions and fairs. The young people who entered the engineering contests shown on these pages have discovered something important about engineering: It's creative and it's fun!

Some of the contests are pretty wacky, like the National Rube Goldberg™ Machine Contest, named for a cartoonist who drew weird, incredibly complicated contraptions that performed simple tasks. In 1996 the task set by the Rube Goldberg™ competition, held each year at Purdue University in West Lafayette, Indiana, was to get a coin into a bank—in no *fewer* than twenty steps! Students from the University of Wisconsin didn't win the 1996 contest, but they had a great time building a machine they called Money Grubbers (bottom).

In the large photo (facing page), radio-controlled "robo-gladiators" built by high school students fight during a U.S. FIRST robotic competition in New Hampshire. The brainchild of engineer Dean Kamen, the contest is a national elimination tournament that calls on kids' inventive and engineering skills as well as their desire to win. Kamen hopes that the U.S. FIRST contest will be featured on TV someday—like the Super Bowl or the World Series—and will inspire kids everywhere to create useful inventions.

Building the future. *Elementary school participants in Project Create (top) showcase underwater communities at a fair in Orlando, Florida. The Future City Competition™, which is part of National Engineers Week every year throughout the United States, has students use a computer game to design an energy-efficient city and then build a three-dimensional model of it (above center).*

College contests. *Engineering students at Purdue University perform last-minute checks on their solar car before a race in Australia (above). At George Washington University in Washington, D.C., students smooth out the rough edges of their canoe before entering it in a national concrete canoe competition (right).*

The History of Engineering

Engineering is a profession that contributes to making life better for large numbers of people. For example, Roman engineers built aqueducts to carry clean water from faraway hills into the city. Beginning around 300 B.C. and continuing for five centuries, the results were an eight-hundred-mile system, some of which ran on top of multileveled, arched bridges like the one in the photo at top right. Part of civilized life for ancient Romans was enjoying outdoor baths—thanks to engineers.

The Roman engineers were not the first inventive people to design structures for carrying water into human settlements. Simple aqueducts had been devised in the Middle East even earlier. But Romans are considered the first civil engineers. They built extensive systems of bridges and roads to move their armies and enlarge their empire.

Engineers build systems to carry water, ease travel, and house people. From putting up the first huts to erecting the highest skyscrapers, they have built shelters and workplaces. The structure may be a cozy house or a beautiful place in which to practice religion. In medieval Europe, engineers found ways to make cathedrals structurally sound *and* beautiful, like Notre-Dame de Paris, in France (center). Built during the late twelfth and early thirteenth centuries, Notre Dame has pointed Gothic arches, which are very strong. It also has structural supports called flying buttresses—

Marvels of engineering. *Through the centuries engineers have used building materials and their own ingenuity to move water through aqueducts (top), build houses of worship (center), and harness the energy of wind power (above left) and human muscle (above right).*

TREVITHICK'S,
PORTABLE STEAM ENGINE.

Catch me who can.

Mechanical Power Subduing
Animal Speed.

GUN SMITH

Famous engineers. James Watt (above) perfected the steam engine. America's first president, George Washington (left), called for engineering schools. Inventor Eli Whitney (below) created machinery with interchangeable parts.

the curved projections at the back of the building. The design of the buttresses allowed cathedral builders to put up taller, thinner walls adorned with stained-glass windows.

Through the centuries engineers have invented tools, put up buildings, bridged rivers, and tunneled through rock. They have harnessed the energy of wind using windmills (facing page, bottom left), and they have devised machinery that harnesses human energy, such as the Chinese treadwheel detailed in an eighteenth-century woodcut (facing page, bottom right). Similar wheels using moving water, instead of people, are still in use at mills around the world.

Beginning in the 1700s engineers began to figure out ways to use the energy in the steam released by boiling water. They developed engines that converted steam energy into mechanical energy. James Watt, a Scotsman, is often credited with inventing the steam engine. But his real accomplishment—one that changed the world—was perfecting the design of the engine so that it could use steam power effectively. This new steam technology led to the design and manufacturing of self-powered engines such as coal carts that moved on tracks in the mines (bottom).

Historians often cite the development of the steam engine as the start of a period in modern history called the industrial revolution. This revolution, which began in England but quickly spread to Europe and America, transformed the way people worked and how they got from place to place. A major contributor to this change was

Engineering partners. *Washington A. Roebling (far left) became seriously ill while he was overseeing the construction of New York's Brooklyn Bridge (center left), which his father, John A. Roebling, had designed. Washington's wife, Emily (near left), learned about engineering and finished the job.*

the steam locomotive, introduced by Richard Trevithick. In 1804 Trevithick applied Watt's steam technology to transportation. The first U.S. railway train ran in 1825, and this newfangled way to get from place to place caught on fast. By 1869 a transcontinental railway line stretched across the United States, all the way from the Atlantic to the Pacific.

This period of rapid technological change created a need to formally educate engineers. The first engineering school opened in Paris in 1794. Several years later President George Washington called for the creation of an engineering school in the United States. In 1824 the first civilian U.S. engineering school, Rensselaer Polytechnic Institute, opened its doors in Troy, New York.

With the development of steam power and new transportation systems, innovative ways to build and manufacture things were also implemented. In the United States an inventor named Eli Whitney came up with the idea of parts that could be used in making many different products. Eventually, interchangeable parts would lead to mass production of everything from automobiles to weapons.

Assembly line. *Henry Ford's economical manufacturing methods (above) allowed him to* lower *prices. A Ford cost $780 in 1910. By 1924 the price had dropped to $290. At that price, even people with modest incomes could buy one.*

Important innovators. *George Westinghouse (near right) founded the company that bears his name and was one of the first engineers to use the assembly line (center right). He's famous for harnessing the energy of electricity. Thomas Edison (far right) invented the lightbulb— and hundreds of other useful devices.*

Forms of communication were changing, too. Samuel Morse (facing page, second row, right) invented the telegraph in 1837, making it possible to send long-distance messages rapidly. Huge steamships, including the *Great Eastern* (facing page, second row, left), laid an undersea cable from Europe to America in 1866.

Engineers have been busy in the twentieth century, too. During the 1900s Henry Ford (facing page, bottom) combined various technologies in a way that changed the world. He used interchangeable parts, and he devised a mechanical system of conveyor belts to move his product, an automobile, through a factory assembly line. Using this method, Ford could make many more cars than his competition could. The result: the affordable Model T. Introduced in 1908, the Model T Ford was the first car that working-class people were able to buy.

Cars, trains, rapid communication. Sounds a lot like the world we live in, doesn't it? But there were some major differences—no television, for one. Engineer Vladimir Zworykin (right) is holding a device that changed that. The 1929 version of the cathode ray tube on his lap eventually evolved into the television screen.

Going up. *You wouldn't easily get to the top of the 1,454-foot Sears Tower in Chicago (above), or of any skyscraper, without an elevator. Elevator design is still based on the 1850s invention of Elisha Otis and the pulley that lowered and raised the elevator (inset above).*

Great Feats of the Twentieth Century

Technology builds on technology—so new inventions often lead to new products and record-breaking achievements. Can you think of other engineering wonders that exist today?

GOLDEN GATE BRIDGE
1937

TELEVISION
1931

APOLLO MOON LANDING
1969

PANAMA CANAL
1914

APPLICATION SATELLITES
1957

ARTIFICIAL HEART
1967

AIRCRAFT CARRIER
1958

TRANS-ALASKA PIPELINE
1977

NUCLEAR POWER
1950s

FIBER-OPTIC COMMUNICATIONS
1977

COMBINE HARVESTER
1975

GENETIC ALTERATIONS
1981

EMPIRE STATE BUILDING
1931

CAT SCAN
1970s

MICROPROCESSOR
1958

JUMBO JETS
1969

COMPOSITE MATERIALS
1985

AQUA-LUNG ™
1943

LASERS
1956

COMPUTER-AIDED DESIGN
1970s

SYDNEY OPERA HOUSE
1973

BULLET TRAINS
1971

ELECTRON MICROSCOPE
1931

SYNTHETIC FIBER
1930s

Movie Magic

Engineers who work in the movie business can picture amazing things in their heads and make them happen on screen. But there are a lot of steps between imagination and what you actually see in a movie theater. Let's go behind the scenes to see motion picture engineers at work.

Jumanji is the story of two kids who play a magic board game that makes animals such as lions and rhinos come dramatically to life right inside their house. Many of the amazing animatronic special effects in the movie were the work of Amalgamated Dynamics, Inc. (ADI), of Los Angeles, California. Animatronics is the science of engineering models that move following the commands of built-in electronic programs. Above, ADI director Tom Woodruff and engineer George Bernota are working on the circuits that will bring a lion's head roaring to life. In the background, Alec Gillis, ADI's other director, checks some of the wiring. Those are George Bernota's hands fiddling in the "guts" of an animatronic spider in the small photo at left.

The creatures in *Jumanji* were both anima-

Bringing a lion to life. On his screen, Industrial Light & Magic computer wizard Carl Frederick combines the pieces that create an animated lion for the movie Jumanji *(above). At right are four digital shot breakdowns that together create a scene of the lion strolling in a hallway (from the top): the empty hallway; a "wire-frame" model created with the computer to show how the image will take up space; the wire-frame placed on top of the hallway image; and the drawn-in lion come to life.*

tronic models and digital animated drawings that were created by another company, Industrial Light & Magic (ILM), in San Rafael, California. ILM is world-famous for its state-of-the-art computerized special effects. ILM designers have won dozens of Academy Awards for Best Visual Effects and Technical Achievement. Above, ILM computer graphics supervisor Carl Frederick works at his terminal, combining the different parts of an animated scene. You might think that Carl Frederick's education was in art and film. In fact, he studied mathematics and computers. He's a computer engineer!

Robotics

Have you ever wanted a robot to help you out with the tasks of daily life? You may not have a personal robot helper yet, but robots already play a major role in manufacturing things you use at home. In Japan a robot traffic cop helps keep vehicles moving safely (top right). The Japanese name for the robot is *anzen taro,* or "traffic boy." Another Japanese robot serves the Oobuchi family at the Grazie Italian restaurant in Tokyo (bottom left). The waiter robot, named Ken-Chan, is engineered to speak as well as serve; its phrases include "Welcome" and "You all look happy." Robots of the future will take the place of people in doing dangerous jobs, including fire fighting. In Utah a firefighter demonstrates body positions as an engineer works on a robot that imitates human motion (top left). Robots may also take the place of workers in fields such as construction. In the photo below (bottom right), a civil engineer works on designing software that will allow robots to build walls, then paint them.

Robots at work. *Robotic arms assemble high-tech toilet seats at Toto Aqua Electronics in Japan (top left). Engineers test the Mars Rover, which will be used to explore the red planet's surface, in the rugged terrain of Death Valley (top right). A glass panel separates Massachusetts Institute of Technology student Chris Foley from Eddie, the wall-climbing, suction-footed robot he designed in the MIT Artificial Intelligence Laboratory (above left). A robot reads music and plays piano at a science expo in Japan (above right).*

High Tech

The new equipment, techniques, and communication systems such as the Internet that engineers design change lives for the better. At left, a patient undergoes laser eye surgery. Using the thin, concentrated beams of light, surgeons can repair eye injuries such as detached retinas with amazing precision.

In the top photo, a technician uses bar codes like the ones scanned in your grocery store to track samples of human DNA (deoxyribonucleic acid). The black bars and white spaces on bar codes are read by a beam of infrared light from the device the technician holds. DNA, a substance found in human tissue, carries genetic information. Every human has unique DNA. It can be used in many ways, from medical research to analyzing evidence in crime cases.

You might not think that playing with Legos™ could lead to a career in engineering. But why not? Building with the toy blocks, you use design and problem-solving skills, the ability to imagine in three dimensions, and patience. Now meet Dr. LegoHead. Developed By Rick Borovoy (center) at the MIT Media Laboratory, a place for research about new information technology, the "intelligent" toy allows kids to use electronics to make it move and talk.

On-line. *At Sprint's Network Management Center in Reston, Virginia (above), communications experts work at banks of terminals as they monitor Internet transmissions and flow of data for private companies. If you "surf" through the information on the World Wide Web, chances are these people are helping. Sprint is the largest Internet access provider in the world.*

In a grain of sand. *Silicon (above left), the basic ingredient in sand, is used to make computer chips such as in the "clean room" in Research Triangle Park, North Carolina (above right). At the University of Haifa in Israel, a technician works on installing microelectronics components in an automated artificial hand (top). Krista Caudill, who is deaf and blind, tests a finger-spelling robotic hand at the Alfred I. duPont Institute in Wilmington, Delaware (above center).*

International Engineering

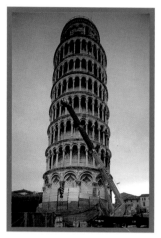

Throughout the world, engineers work to build new structures, improve the quality of life, and solve problems caused by pollution or age. The Tower of Pisa (left), completed six centuries ago, has long been nicknamed the Leaning Tower. Over time it tilted seventeen feet out of vertical as the soft ground beneath it settled unevenly. This tower in northern Italy has been restored by engineers to keep it from tilting further.

High tech is worldwide. In Hong Kong a technician checks the quality of semiconductors (top right). Beneath the English Channel, earth and rocks are removed during the excavation of the Channel Tunnel, nicknamed the Chunnel (second from top, right). Now in daily use, the thirty-one-mile-long tunnel has a twenty-four-mile underwater section, the world's longest.

Technology also has worldwide side effects. When coal and oil are burned to provide power for manufacturing, chemicals are released that combine with water in clouds to produce acid rain. Acid rain damages crops, buildings, and monuments. A restoration specialist in Venice, Italy, cleans a statue harmed by acid rain (second from bottom, right).

In China a huge new dam will displace millions of people from their homes. Some experts say the dam is needed to control the Yangtze River's flooding, but the financial and human cost is very high. Technology can also be helpful, however. At the International Rice Research Institute in the Philippines, a genetic engineer works to develop a kind of rice that can be grown easily to feed hungry people (bottom right).

Engineers work at Carajás Mine in Brazil, the largest iron-ore mine in the world (above). Construction workers crowd the site of the Yangtze River Dam in China (right). The dam will be the world's largest. A reservoir will flood land behind the dam, forcing a million people to move.

Some Noteworthy Engineers

Sometimes engineers' names are linked with inventions—like James Watt's with the steam engine. Other engineers remain anonymous because they solve problems as part of a team. Others may be well-known in their fields but unfamiliar to nonengineers. Here are some important engineers.

BENJAMIN WRIGHT

Called the father of civil engineering, Wright, who lived from 1770–1842, was chief engineer of the Erie Canal, which made travel and trade possible from Lake Erie to the Hudson River.

THOMAS TELFORD

This Scottish engineer built the world's first suspension bridge, completed in Wales in 1826. Telford also created elevated roads for better drainage and covered them with large paving stones.

SYLVANUS THAYER

Thayer pioneered engineering education in America by adapting French educational practices to such new schools as Thayer School of Civil Engineering, which he founded at Dartmouth College.

CHARLES STARK DRAPER

Known as Doc, Draper was the inventor of modern navigation systems. He developed practical systems for long-distance navigation for aircraft, space vehicles, strategic missiles, and submarines.

LILLIAN M. GILBRETH

Collaborating with her husband, Gilbreth worked on time-and-motion studies designed to help companies become more efficient. This industrial engineer also raised twelve children.

MARIO MOLINA

The first Latino Nobel Prize winner for chemistry, in 1995, chemical engineer Molina was the first scientist to suggest that man-made chemicals were damaging Earth's ozone layer.

MILDRED S. DRESSELHAUS

A physicist, engineer, and National Medal of Science winner, Dresselhaus has been a member of the Massachusetts Institute of Technology's electrical engineering faculty for more than thirty years.

NAM P. SUH

A professor of mechanical engineering at the Massachusetts Institute of Technology, Suh originated a branch of science called tribology, the study of how and why materials wear out.

OSCAR SUROS

As manager of engineering and architecture for the Port Authority of New York, this structural engineer is responsible for maintaining structures such as the George Washington Bridge and the World Trade Center.

LONNIE REID

A mechanical engineer, Reid headed NASA's Internal Fluid Mechanics Division. He also studied the flow of air through aircraft engines to develop quieter and cleaner equipment for passenger planes.

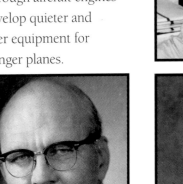

HAROLD ROSEN (left) and JOHN PIERCE (right)
These 1995 winners of the Charles Stark Draper Prize—the National Academy of Engineering's highest honor—designed, developed, and produced pioneering communications satellite networks in the 1960s. At Bell Laboratories, Pierce developed and published the first practical engineering calculations for space communication. After reading Pierce's work, Rosen worked at Hughes Aircraft to design a satellite communications system.

JACK S. KILBY (left) and ROBERT N. NOYCE (right)
In 1990 these engineers shared the Charles Stark Draper Prize for co-inventing the integrated circuit, better known as the semiconductor microchip. Their invention made miniaturization of computers possible and helped lead the world into the information age. Noyce's company provided integrated circuits to the space program for the onboard computer in the *Gemini* space capsule.

GRACE MURRAY HOPPER

While in the U.S. Navy WAVEs during World War II, Hopper developed operating programs for Mark I, an early computer. She wrote COBOL, the first English-language programming system.

MAE C. JEMISON

A chemical engineer, Jemison became the first African American woman in space in 1992. She also holds a doctorate in medicine from Cornell University. Today Jemison works as an educator.

JOHN B. SLAUGHTER

A specialist in electrical and environmental engineering, as well as physics, Slaughter has been a director of the National Science Foundation and is president of Occidental College.

MARY ROSS

A researcher in aerospace development and design concepts for interplanetary space travel, Native American Mary Ross, who is Cherokee, launched her career as a mathematician and teacher.

You Can Be an Engineer!

Do you ever wonder if the math and science you're learning at school is useful? Kids like Justin Cox, right, participating in a Young Technocrats engineering program in Washington, D.C., discover that math and science are a lot more than just solving equations on paper. For engineers, math and science are tools.

Engineers apply existing technology to real-world problems in new ways—or they invent new technologies that no one has thought of before. They begin with their imaginations and then use tools including math and science to make the dreams come true.

As Justin Cox discovered from his Young Technocrats experience, engineering often involves taking things apart and putting them back together in new ways. It's like putting a puzzle together. Does that idea get the gears in your brain turning? Then you're already thinking like an engineer.

"I always wondered, when I was growing up, *How does this doorknob work?* or thought, *Let me take this apart and see how it works,*" says NASA astronaut Jan Davis, a mechanical engineer. "If you're like that, engineering is right up your alley."

There are dozens of programs to help young people learn about the many branches of the engineering profession. To find out more about some of them, turn the page.

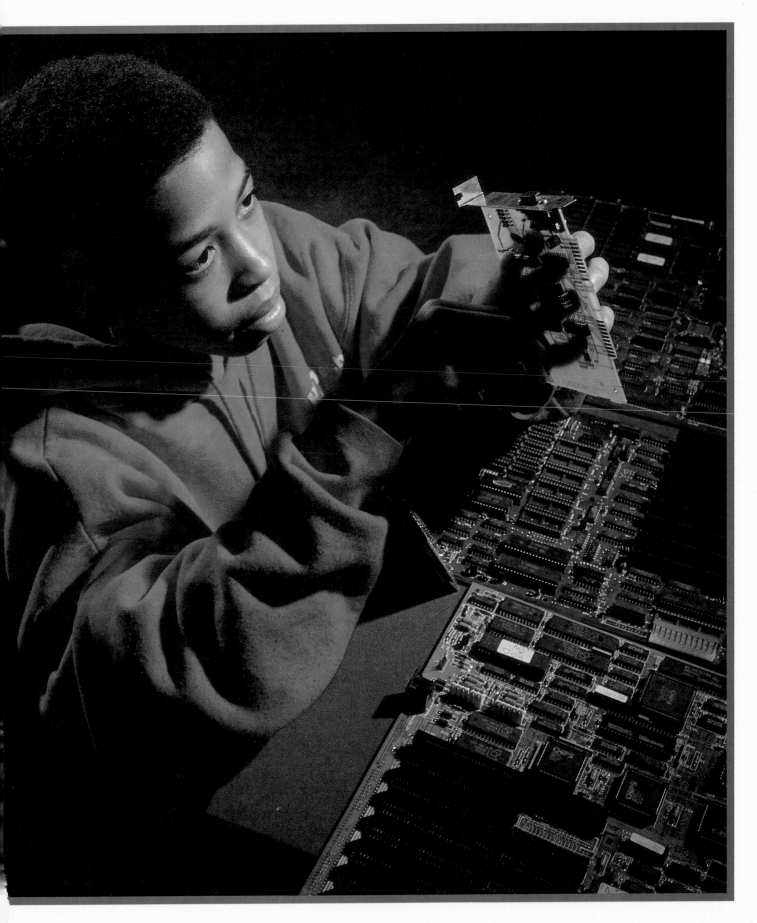

Other Sources of Information

PROFESSIONAL AND EDUCATIONAL ORGANIZATIONS:

American Association for the Advancement of Science
1333 H Street NW
Washington, DC 20005

The world's largest general science professional organization. Write for informational pamphlets and educational materials.

American Chemical Society
1155 16th Street NW
Washington, DC 20036

National membership organization of chemists of all kinds, including chemical engineers. Write for information about programs and publications for students.

American Institute of Aeronautics and Astronautics
Department JG
370 L'Enfant Promenade SW
Washington, DC 20024

Write for information about careers in aerospace engineering.

American Society for Engineering Education
1818 N Street NW, Suite #600
Washington, DC 20036

Organizes postdoctoral and faculty programs. Publishes Prism Magazine *on Engineering.*

American Society of Civil Engineers
Education Division
1801 Alexander Bell Drive
Reston, VA 20191-4400

Write for detailed information about youth programs and careers in civil engineering.

American Society of Mechanical Engineers
Education Department
345 East 47th Street
New York, NY 10017

Write for detailed information about careers in mechanical engineering.

Center for Children and Technology
Educational Development Corporation
96 Morton Street
New York, NY 10014

Write to receive the free Center for Children and Technology Newsletter.

Institute of Electrical and Electronics Engineers (IEEE)
345 East 47th Street
New York, NY 10017

Provides educational information about careers in electrical engineering, including jobs working with computers.

International Society for Technology in Education
1787 Agate Street
Eugene, OR 97403

Check out this organization's home page on the Internet at iste@oregon.uoregon.edu *for information about programs to bring technology into the classroom.*

Junior Engineering Technical Society (JETS)
1420 King Street, Suite 405
Alexandria, VA 22314-2715

A national organization dedicated to encouraging students to choose engineering as a career. Conducts academic programs and design competitions. Write for brochures, videotapes, and books.

National Aeronautics and Space Administration
Education Division
Code FEP
300 E Street NW
Washington, DC 20546-0001

Oversees the U.S. space program. Write for a wide variety of educational pamphlets and materials.

National Society of Black Engineers
Programs Division
1454 Duke Street
Alexandria, VA 22314

Offers information and a brochure on K–12 educational programs designed to encourage young African Americans to study math, science, and technology.

National Society of Professional Engineers

Education Foundation
1420 King Street
Alexandria, VA 22314-2715

The national membership organization for all engineering professionals. Write for educational pamphlets and materials.

Society of Hispanic Professional Engineers

5400 Olympic Blvd., Suite 306
Los Angeles, CA 90022

Promotes engineering opportunities for Hispanics. Publishes national newsletter, Hispanic Engineer magazine, and develops local outreach programs.

Society of Women Engineers

120 Wall Street
New York, NY 10005

A professional organization of women engineers. One of the group's goals is to encourage young women to study science and pursue careers in science and technology. Write for more information.

SPECIAL EVENTS:

National Engineers Week

P.O. Box 1020
Sewickley, PA 15143

Write for information about the annual week-long event in February that celebrates the work of engineers. National Engineers Week was founded in 1951 by the Society of Professional Engineers.

National Rube Goldberg™ Machine Contest

Purdue University
West Lafayette, IN 47907-1132

A fun, creative annual invention contest named for a cartoonist who drew incredibly complicated contraptions that performed simple tasks.

U.S. FIRST, The Competition

340 Commercial Street
Manchester, NH 03101

A national tournament that pits radio-controlled mechanical devices against each other in elimination matches. The acronym signifies For Inspiration and Recognition of Science and Technology.

MUSEUMS:

Boston Computer Museum

300 Congress Street
Boston, MA 02210

National Building Museum

401 F Street NW
Washington, DC 20001

National Air & Space Museum

Smithsonian Institution
Washington, DC 20560

For information about museums in your area, write to:

Association of Science Technology Centers

1025 Vermont Avenue NW
Suite 500
Washington, DC 20005

PHOTO CREDITS